Fight Songs for the Underdogs

Selected Poems by Dan Denton

Luchador Press
Big Tuna, Texas

Copyright © Dan Denton, 2025
First Edition: 1 3 5 7 9 10 8 6 4 2
ISBN: 979-8-89975-010-6
LCCN: 2025939358

Author photo: PhotoDave Photography

"For 2½ years, I had the distinct honor of sharing a union steward desk with Dan. I had barely known him when we started, but I learned to love him like a brother. Not in the union "brotherhood" sense, but in the ACTUAL brother sense. We fought about ideals and solutions to problems. We fought over the layout of our desk, and who got which drawers to file papers in. But we were on opposing shifts, so we only fought for a few short minutes before one of us had to go home and the other had to start his shift. Occasionally, I would find a scrap of paper with a few scribbled lines of a poem on it, lost under our shared keyboard or on the floor under our shared chair. And the realization of who Dan truly is and was would bowl me over again and again and again.

I have never met someone who has such an ability to make me feel so much through a poem. Not in the "emotional" sense, but the "cold, drizzly, grey morning, while crunching the fresh, but already dirty snow under my work boots" sense. The factory life ain't easy by any means. Dan has a seemingly never-ending list of ways to describe how much of a toll it takes on a person, mentally, physically, and emotionally.

Dan has a way of sticking the all-seeing eye of his needle like words straight into the closest open vein under a sore blue-collar neck, and paying homage to the grit under the fingernails, the grease on the arms, the blisters on heels, and the cuts on the back of hands that keep both the factory and working class turning. The mundane is shown as exactly that, but with glimmers of hope, purpose, pride, and strength. The drudgery & monotony is all for a reason, and a dignified paycheck, and that somehow makes it worth it. He makes me feel like I am not alone, in a way and a life that no one else I've ever read can."

-"Big" John Mohr - former UAW Chief Steward, afternoon shift, JL Wrangler Assembly- current supplier quality inspector on afternoon shift

"In his tradition of the poet-as-prophet and the worker-as-witness, this labor-loving poet stands at the confluence of sweat and stanza, where calloused hands and unflinching verse carve truth into the fabric of working-class life. Dan Denton's poetry does not romanticize the labor struggle—it lives it. Forged in union halls, picket lines, and long nights under fluorescent light. His voice rises not from theory but from practice: from organizing, from resisting, from refusing to let silence smother solidarity. Each line is a ledger of real lives, real costs, and hard-won dignity, echoing with the rhythm of machinery and the heartbeat of collective power. This is poetry that doesn't flinch, that refuses polish when grit is honest. With authenticity etched into every syllable, his poetry reminds us that the revolution is not only organized—it is sung."

-Jody Russell, Proud UAW Member

Acknowledgments

Some of these poems found a home in other print journals prior to this one, and the author is eternally grateful for that. Thank you to *Toledo Streets Newspaper*, *The Rusty Truck*, *Lost, Long Gone, Forgotten Records*, *The Broadway Bards Anthology*, and *Poet Plant Press*.

Special thanks to Osage Arts Community, Luchador Press and editor Jason Ryberg for giving these sweat stained words a nice home they can be proud of.

To my many friends, factory brothers and sisters, loved ones, artist comrades and supporters

and to Roque Dalton for teaching me that poetry is for everyone. Especially so for the underdogs in life.

Table of Contents

From *One for Toledo* Streets Newspaper

From *C'mon Man Let's Talk About It*

From *Junkyard Heart*
(The Lunch Bucket Brigade, 2025.)

From *Hope is a Lost Dog*
(The Lunch Bucket Brigade, 2023.)

From *Love Song for Toledo,* (The Lunch Bucket Brigade, 2023)

Other Selected Work

The rain zigzagged across the show window in torrents and black gleaming umbrellas with frantic legs beneath were blown past. Market Street lamps were wet golden blobs dripping futile little puddles of light that made no difference to the black, wet night...

-*Dance Night*, Dawn Powell

"And the commercials would have sickened a goat raised on barbed wire and broken beer bottles."

-*The Long Goodbye*, Raymond Chandler

To my children, Spenser, Iris and Finn. I was a poet and a man before I was a father, but I'm a greater one of each because of you three.

Eat Your Beats Kids

boom bah tish ooo aaah
eat your Beats kids

as if you could walk into
any thrift store in town
and walk out of there
posing as punk
as if your mom and dad
could buy you street cred
as if you could live a junkie life
without any of the junk

shut up!
and eat your Beats kids

as if the communist manifesto
makes any goddamn sense in the suburbs
as if Richard Nixon never tried to smother
your hippie parents
or choke the life out of
the back alley beatniks

as if found poems from hotel Bibles
had any soul
as if the shit music playing in elevators
has ever threatened Miles Davis

ha ha ha a ha ha
shut up!
and eat your Beats kids

as if the Virgin Mary wasn't a symbol of pedophilia
as if your plastic heart has never raced
while kissing the cigarette burns
on a hooker's tits

as if words from a thesaurus could fuck Ginsberg's
ghost and make poems drop like bombs
as if Prozac was proof that you were an artist
as if Huncke wasn't the fucking mayor
of 42nd street

shut up!
and eat your Beats kids

as if the blues could be captured by a compact disc
as if jazz lived in Beverly Hills
as if psychiatrists could wave a fucking magic wand
and pronounce you a writer
as if we needed permission from our government
to celebrate poetry for a month
as if street poets smoking down
dropped cigarette butts
ever gave a damn about April

as if capitalism hadn't already murdered god

ha ha ha a ha ha
boom boom bah hiss tisk
eat your Beats kids

A Little Fire Left

Hey Maestro
can you paint me a picture
a picture of my life
and I hate
to tell an artist
how to do their work
but could you paint
a little less sunshine
and maybe
not so many
bright colors?

and since we're
depicting my life
we probably should
throw a little sand on it
paint a little more night

let me look
not bad
not bad Maestro

but let's paint
a little flame
right here in the corner

despite the dark and the dirt
despite those women over there
and that train wreck over here

in spite of that stack of soul sucking jobs
and those years I flirted with the devil
despite those cold streets there
where I made my bed
despite the empty moments
despite the empty years

despite the dead zones
despite all the wounds-
many self inflicted
despite nearly drowning in madness
despite the bloody noses
despite the starving wolves that circle
despite the nights that called me away
despite the days that choked me

despite playing a game
that I know I'll never win
despite knowing this is a lie
that it's always been a lie

despite the black hole
in the middle
of it all
despite myself
despite this collage of chaos

let's paint a little flame
right here in the corner
because there's still
a little fire left maestro

there's a gun in this hand
and a cheap ballpoint in the other
and in between them
is still a little fire
and that's more
than one should expect
from a life like this one

Some Days

some days life
is like running a week old razor
over a sunburned face

or like re-living
the same two seconds prior to a crash
the moment you realize it's too late to swerve
and you're bracing for an impact
that happens in slow motion

it's like rubbing antiseptic soap
into work-worn hands,
feeling the sting
in every crack, split
and open sore -
some that you can't see
but the soap still finds them

it's like slowly peeling a band-aid off
the hairy part of your arm
like getting out of bed with a stiff back
like having a low grade migraine
like having a mild toothache
like walking all day with a blister on your heel

it's like leaving a bar at closing time
knowing there are three goons waiting outside
to kick your ass
and walking out there anyway

the best of the worst days
still hurt like hell

the toughest amongst us
get up earlier than they have to
and live it anyway

Another Morning in the Shit Show

how many mornings have I sat outside rusty buildings
smoking cigarettes
and counting down the hours
of a long mundane work shift?

how many cigarettes have I burned down
listening to the silence of my dejected coworkers?

how many days have I spent
watching the rain drops fall-
nursing my broken knees-
knowing that I didn't have to wind up here?

how many more packs of cigarettes
do I have to rip open
standing on dirty concrete
wishing the weekend would hurry up
and get here
even though I know
they'll make me work then too

this morning the bosses ran around
screaming to keep the assembly line running
as if their lives depended on it
I stepped outside and smiled
enjoying the ultimate game of factory worker's
chicken-

will I breakdown before I retire?

I lit another cigarette
outside another factory
knowing that this place
will not be the death of me

The Lies of Morning

every morning I wake up gritting my teeth
determined to have a great day-
my back groans when I bend to put on my shoes
you'll feel better when you start moving I tell myself
I force a smile when I look in the bathroom mirror
everything is going to be alright
I search til I find a little twinkle in my eyes

I listen to good music on the drive to work
singing along with the radio
tapping a beat on the steering wheel
when one of my favorite tunes
pours out of the speakers
I claim it as a sign-
it's gonna be a good day

I joke with my coworkers
sip my coffee and watch as my resolve
slowly erodes with the tedium
by lunch time my lower back protests
sending tingling numbness stabbing
into my left butt cheek and
the factory floor is as unforgiving as
a Republican governor

when I limp out of the gates at the end of my shift
I wonder why I ever bothered trying
to convince myself of the morning's lies

Turn Down the Volume

the words of yesterday's poets
echo
in tomorrow's thoughts

only the seagulls know
as they circle
dead parking lots
squawking and crying
praying over lost french fries

what if the junkie on the corner
was Jim Morrison in a past life
what if the junkie on the corner
was my brother in this life
what if the junkie on the corner
is Michael the Archangel
and he's traded away his golden trumpet
for a little smack

       Our Father, who art in Heaven

I met the Son of God
in the psych ward
back in '02

       ...hallowed be thy name

he said razor blades
liked to dance on his wrists
he traded me a blessing for a cigarette
maybe that's why
I've survived this long

the American Revolutionary War
is still being fought in the streets
and freedom sometimes still requires
a dead body

the silent tears of lost children
keep me awake at night
all the Saints are still dead
sparrows peck at the dirt

the rapture has been postponed
as long as Jesus
is still trading parables for Marlboros

skeletons dance in the streets
and it's all so loud
sometimes I wish that I was deaf
so I could get a little sleep

Bury My Heart in the Gutter

how much longer will I have to endure
cable television and paid infomercials

how much longer will I have to endure
24 hour news channels

how much longer will I have to drive
through small towns with clean streets
and rows of American flags

or drive through suburbia
with its shiny cop cars and shiny cops
carrying shiny guns

how much longer will I have to live
counting down the days
until they put Planet Earth on the endangered
species list

how much longer
I do not know
but when the end comes
bury my heart in the gutter

bury it where the pimps and the street preachers work-
near the corners
where junkies and hustlers share space

bury it in an alley behind a dumpster
or under a bridge where the stray dogs live

take me back home
where 3 dollars and 75 cents
will buy a bottle of strong cheap wine

the gutter
where I found the people that god NEVER loved

the gutter
where I learned that crack cocaine is both
the devil
and the angel of life

where I learned that fucking and fighting
are the coping mechanisms of damaged people

and that there's nothing softer
than the maternal instincts
of a kind-hearted whore

where I learned
that when you have nothing-
there is freedom

where I learned
that hell is a real place
and you don't have to die to go there

where I learned
that I am more than my addictions

and where I learned
the most valuable lesson of all-
that the same moon that shines on Wall Street
is visible from the gutter
if you're just wise enough
to look up once in a while

my friend
you may not understand
but when my nightmare ends-
bury my heart where it first came alive-
right smack dab in the middle
of the motherfuckin' gutter

From the chapbook, *Give Us This Day Our Daily Grind: an ode to the American Factory Worker* (The Lunch Bucket Brigade, 2020.)

Give Us This Day Our Daily Grind:
an Ode to the American Factory Worker

everyday something hurts
your back, your knees, your feet
your shoulders, your arms, your hands
and on the bad days it all hurts
and you limp in and out of the factory

it's like that in a lot of factories
not just the one I go to everyday
there's an army of American factory workers
punching in and out
every eight or ten or twelve hours

we know our trades are slowly dying off
we're being choked to death by corporate greed
it's cheaper to build our products in Mexico
in Vietnam, in China.
there isn't much glamour in a factory
most of us didn't really plan
to make this our careers anyway
but the factory life gets in your blood
and you get used to that daily grind
and we don't really know what we'd do for work
if the factory shut down

and you wouldn't call it a noble profession
but whole cities have been built around us

they say it's the rust belt now
but most cities wish they had more of us
because when our hours are good
the economy is good and really
we might be the backbone of America
but what do I know
I'm just an ol' factory worker

The Factories That Make Us

we work all day
past what should be the point of exhaustion
doing hard jobs
that over the months and years
make us hard people

we slough through snow or rain
and into the doors of giant buildings
to build stuff for you to buy
so we can buy food
to feed our families

we've spent a lifetime
listening to politicians stump for our votes
promising to look out for our jobs
knowing that they never have
and they never will
they can't
when they're taking money
from the rich people that employ us

we work all day in the smothering heat
while dead fans blow dead air
and sweat seeps through our t- shirts

we punch out on time clocks
toting empty lunch buckets back home

where our televisions are filled with newscasters
that tell us how good
the economy is doing

we work overtime on the weekends
and talk about the summer vacations we're planning
and how our kids are doing in school

we're called roughnecks
and auto workers
press operators and die makers

we build the American economy
with our hands and backs
while stocks go down
then up higher
and we just keep punching in
and back out
with tough feet
and strong wills
our blue collars worn with a fierce pride
tough good people
doing hard jobs

at night
we sleep under the sounds of droning air conditioners
only to get up before the sun
to go back to the factories that make us

The Steel Jungle

in an auto plant
where the assembly line snakes through
everywhere you turn
there is constant motion

it's like a steel jungle
the ground a concrete floor
lots of industrial gray paint
yellow safety paint
and a painted blue stripe
to show you where to walk
as you navigate the jungle

when you're new
it's easy to get lost
in two million square feet of activity
though the veterans slip in and out
and through hidden spaces-
they know this jungle
like a roadmap is imbedded
on the back of their eyelids

the steel jungle is alive
just like any jungle is
and it will swallow you up
and spit you out
thirty years after your first day
if you're lucky

the jungle hums and hisses
it squeaks and squeals
and clangs
but if you listen carefully
you can hear the murmured prayers
of a shrinking middle class
rising like steam
from the towering smokestack skeletons
of the steel jungle

The Midwest

where we wear our work ethics
like prideful chips
that sit on our shoulders

where Jesus still has a lot of influence
in political elections

where blue collar is a compliment

where commodities prices are read on the radio
every day at 5pm

where country music is the king

where beer is mass produced

where the American flag is viewed
as a holy relic

the Midwest
where I was born and raised
and where I have spent most of my life

where I have driven past so many abandoned factories
that I've lost all faith
of there being labor unions in Heaven

where I have lost so many friends to overdoses
that I have become convinced
that there is heroin in Heaven

if America was a hand
the Midwest would be the callous
on the palm
just under the index finger

if America was a pair of boots
the Midwest would be the laces
that hold them together

if America was human
the Midwest would be
its heart and soul

City Hues

loud blues music plays
in the cab of my blue pickup truck
my faded blue jeans
and scuffed brown work boots
do nothing to hide
the blue collar that covers
my red neck

I sip black gas station coffee
bought from a blue and yellow Sunoco
where I also bought a yellow banana
so yellow
that it almost looked fake

I drive through
the gray December streets
of my city- Toledo,
a city so tough
that it's residents hardly notice
the black and blue bruises
leftover from NAFTA

my blue eyes see the beauty
of black streets
wet from melting snow
black streets
cracked and pocked with holes

black streets
lined with dirty orange barrels

gray skies
hover above dirty oil refineries
that ejaculate black smoke
that turns into black clouds
that float above my gray city- Toledo
a city so tough
that it hums the blues
but never cries them

The American Dream in 2016

all around the city
and within its 75 mile radius
our alarm clocks go off
in the early morning darkness
we drag ourselves tired and aching
into the factory
and a buzzer sounds
the assembly line lurches
and a thousand people move like clockwork
trading away our healthy years to build Jeeps

there was a time
when Jeeps were only built
in the U.S. of A.
but now they build them in China-
in Brazil and in Italy
it's the new global economy

our t-shirts are made in Vietnam
our jeans born in Mexico
and our feet are tired
in our Chinese made work boots

when the buzzer rings for break time
we text our significant others
on mobile devices
from giant cell phone companies
that pay zero federal taxes

and at the end of the day
we race home to mailboxes
jammed with political flyers
telling us which presidential candidate
our union wants us to vote for
flyers promising they'll protect our jobs
even though we read news everyday
of union jobs
leaving the country

in the evening
many of us relax with cold beers
that are made in breweries
owned by Belgian
and South African corporations-
then we shuffle off to bed

just another regular ole day
of living the American dream

We're Union Men

we drink our coffee black
strong and bitter,
while we stifle yawns
walking into work
carrying lunch buckets

we wear our blue jeans
until they fade
and the pockets become threadbare
and we wear our boots year 'round

we keep our t- shirts longer than we should
and in the winter
we wear long sleeves over them

we let our beards grow long in the winter too
and usually trim them back
in the summer months

we work long hours
when the work is good
providing for our families

we mow our lawns every week
or shovel snow from our driveways

we belch and cuss
and we argue about sports and politics
we lay awake at night
our hands hurting
and our backs and knees too
we worry about work slow downs
bad economies
strikes and being able
to make house payments

we build cars
and houses
and steel girders
drive trucks and buses
pour concrete
and run electrical lines.

we are staunchly middle class
and we're a dying breed.

we are union men
and we're a dying breed

From A Stocking Stuffer for Socialists
(The Lunch Bucket Brigade, 2020.)

Immunity from Terror

1.
I'm numb from years of listening
to radio commercials
and reading faded bumper stickers
on the back of rusty SUVs

my spirit is immune to acts of terror
after two decades of news headlines
of war and bombs and immigration
and refugees
and live telecasts of bombed out bunkers
in Flint and Detroit

NAFTA was an act of terror
the Patriot Act was an act of terror
the Supreme Court ruling on Citizens United
was an act of terror
the 2016 Presidential election
was an act of terror

the government of The United States of America
is a terrorist organization
and the great citizens thereof
don't even realize
that they're being held hostage
by corporate ran media

Jeff Bezos and Mark Zuckerberg
and the Koch Brothers and the Walton Family
are all part of the Illuminati
there is a growing militia of social justice warriors
ready to shout down anyone
that still has the ability to think for themselves

I've grown weary
of sitting on my couch
reading books on anarchy and Marxism
while another election cycle
kicks into high gear

2.
when my heart begins to fail
and my fire starts to dim
and it's finally over for me
don't start any gofundme accounts
to pay my medical bills

let me die broke
with my dignity intact
so I can be welcomed into hell
by Marx and Dalton Trumbo
knowing that I never sold out
for the false promise of a comfortable afterlife

I've Lost Faith in This Reality

I've lost faith in this reality
the universal sound of America
is the droning of lawnmowers
the television is our national symbol
the ability to think for one's self
is more endangered than the bald eagle
yet the bald eagle has more governmental
protections than free-thinking does

I don't want to fight
but all the evil in the system forces me to

the most unsolvable mystery in life is
how do you change the world?

we're all living in a giant man-eating machine
it's hard to tell if anyone is to blame for it anymore
my brothers have been brainwashed
into thinking that I'm the enemy

somehow
freedom became illegal
or maybe it always was

A Weeping Heart

I visited the Lorraine Motel
the place where they killed Dr King
they've turned it into a museum now
and I didn't have a lot of time
but I made sure to see it

I stood outside the railing
looking at Room 306
and the red and white wreath
that hung on the bannister and
I looked on as my heart held back tears

this is the place that Dr Martin Luther King Jr
came to rest
this is the place where he was shot
here
this place

this is where America killed a Nobel Prize winner
this is where they killed a father
this is where they killed a husband
a preacher and an activist
a man that only wanted to be known for
feeding the poor

this is the place where they killed a man
that had been hit in the head with bricks

but marched on anyway
this is the place where they killed a man -
a man that stared hate and evil
straight in the eyes and never flinched

this is where they killed a man
this is where America tried to kill a dream
a movement
where they tried to murder hope
this is the place where they tried to kill a dream
but instead they cemented a legacy
that can never die
here in this place where I now stood
with a weeping heart

Do You Feel Me Bro?

I'm tired of working all day
to stay in place
while the rich work less
& gain more every year
I'm tired of sacrificing time
energy & body
just to survive
you feel me bro?

I'm tired of medical bills
weighing me down
keeping me from
chasing my dreams
while people debate
whether health care
is a human right
we know it is
you feel me bro?

I'm tired of arguing with friends
and people that I love
none of us have anything
& very little hope
of getting anywhere
& while we're fighting
bitching about the poor
getting benefits for nothing

the rich and powerful
are taking more
& we don't even notice
because we're too busy bitching
at each other
you feel me bro?

I'm tired of seeing footage
of poor and middle class soldiers
having their lives fucked up
in some bullshit war
that no one really remembers
why we are fighting anymore
and none of us were too sure why
we were fighting to begin with
you feel me bro?

I'm tired of electing
politicians that do nothing
but keep talking about
doing something
& I'm tired
of the same politicians
getting elected every four years anyway
you feel me bro?

I'm tired of living in a country
with a system
that is designed to help the rich
& fuck everyone else

& I'm tired of being told
that I should be grateful
to have a job
grateful to have a home
grateful for things
that all humans deserve
as if I should kiss the man's ass
for allowing me
to have the necessary
things for surviving
you feel me bro?

& mostly I'm tired
of people being tired
people that refuse
to do anything about it
except bitch
I'm tired of people
talking & talking
& talking
but never doing
stop talking already
it's time to do
you feel me bro?

More Than Money

this cup of coffee I'm holding
I had to work 6 minutes to buy it
and this pack of cigarettes I'll smoke today
that was 16 minutes of my labor
federal taxes?
9.5 hours
all that child support?
that was 15 hours and 42 minutes
I've got arthritis in both knees
and will probably need knee replacements
at some point in my life

the last pair of shoes I bought my son
that took 4 hours and 48 minutes
my work boots?
it took 7 hours and 36 minutes to get those
dinner last night
that cost me a little more than an hour
and our monthly rent
is 40 hours and 24 minutes of work
sometimes when I work too much
my hands hurt so bad
that it's hard to tie my shoes in the morning

my new used car
that someone told me I'm lucky to have
will eventually take me 857 hours and 12 minutes to

pay for
and it is a pretty nice ride
but I'm not sure luck will pay the monthly note
14 hours and 42 minutes of labor will

a used book might take me
14 minutes to obtain
a new one
an hour or more
the raffle tickets I bought yesterday
to support childhood literacy
I worked 28 minutes for them
and the lottery tickets I bought today
cost me 11 and a half minutes
the house we might buy
would take 5,714 hours and 18 minutes
until you add the interest
that makes it 9,523 hours and 48 minutes

and that's my point here friends
my back hurts today
and that reminds me
that everything I've ever bought in life
has cost me more than money

America What is Your Excuse?

I like to wash my truck
in the middle of the pouring rain
I take books to gun fights
I hate seeing unarmed people
engaged in a battle of wits

life is hard
so I only eat soft tacos now

let's be honest
none of us want the economy
to ever be so good
that all the graffiti artists become extinct

America
how in the fuck did we elect W.
over John Kerry back in '04?

am I the only one that ever looks around
and wonders where all of
the guerrilla poets have gone?

America why do we allow our country
to arrest people for giving out water?
when did human compassion become illegal?

America we gotta stop comparing
Presidents
to the second coming of Christ
sometimes when I daydream about
what true freedom must feel like
I wind up drowning in sadness
because most of us will never know

has the American Dream ever been about happiness?
or has it always been about complacency?

America how can we still believe
that hard work will bring success?
John Henry was the hardest working man that ever
lived
he worked himself to death
he died broke
they made a song about him
machines are still stealing our jobs

America how much longer can we pretend to be free?
d.a. levy knew he wasn't
Hunter S. Thompson knew he wasn't
Ernest Hemingway and Sylvia Plath knew they weren't
they're all dead now
they died chasing freedom

America what is your excuse?

Midwestern American Average

I've been playing poker enough
down at the local casino
that sometimes
I get comped free dinners

It's kind of nice
to take home a free pizza
after winning $170
on a 7 hour poker jag
to smoke a jay at 2am
and munch on still warm slices of Americana

or like tonight
when I got stoned in the truck
in the oversized parking lot
then bombed out of the evening tourney
my ace-king suited got smoked by pocket aces
and if that last line ain't a chapter in my memoir
then I ain't been true to myself

that free- ironically named 'jackpot' burger
with grilled shrooms and onions
a pound of fries
comfort food
but so average
so American average

midwestern American average
like growing up in downstate Illinois
with at least one relative that has a farm
like spit-shined cowboy boots on an Iowa Saturday night
like ranch dressing in Indiana
like John Grisham novels on Sunday morning
New York Times bestseller lists

midwestern and average
like Stauffer's mac n cheese for Monday night dinner
in February in Toledo

average
like tuxedo t-shirts
in the beer aisle
of the Wal-Mart Supercenter
in Altoona, PA

midwestern U.S.A. Average
like being one cancer scare away
from losing it all

U.S.A. average
like having only one abortion clinic open
in your entire state
if any

U.S.A average
like billion-dollar for-profit hospital offices
on riverfront property

in cities
that are losing the fight against the new NAFTA

average
like brightly lit casinos
standing on the yonder hill
next to the crumbling freeway
two exits past
double digit unemployment rates
and whole neighborhoods
that are barely staying alive
with a free lunch ticket

How American Are You?

as American as fat dumb chain restaurant-
pie eating white people
telling 4th of July jokes
to a young black waitress
as American as that waitress' fake laugh

as American as claw machines full of plastic toys
as American as plastic toys
as American as union t-shirts made in China

as American as watching parades on television
as American as the soulless pop country music
piped into soulless Frisch's Big Boy diners on the
4th of July

as American as a poet watching from the corner booth
as American as a poet eating
apple pie a la mode on the 4th of July
and sipping black coffee from a red coffee mug

as American as American flag swim shorts on the
4th of July
as American as Lee Greenwood
as American as central air conditioning ignoring
climate change

as American as retired people
bussing tables at the Big Boy on the night shift
of a national holiday

as American as American flags on
pick up trucks with Vietnam veteran hats
on the dashboard
as American as Vietnam Veterans
eating chicken fried steak with white gravy
at the local Big Boy diner
all alone at 9pm on the 4th of July

As American as being too dumb to cry
about any of it

One for the Unemployed Elvis Impersonators

tourist streets are empty
and dead
streetlights shine
a gravestone silhouette

America on house arrest
counting flowers
on toilet paper squares

politicians scream
in ever louder sound waves
relentless madness
rolls through town squares

I watch from the window
my television marching a circus cadence
peanuts sold as
middle class bailouts

underneath the cacophony
I whisper nothing prayers
I hope the safety net catches
all of the unemployed
Elvis impersonators

Emergency Room at Midnight in Toledo

young would-be mother cries
young would-be father struggles to console
whispered words between silent sobs

man lays on floor
rolls with pain
groans and grunts

cops watch front door
"Sir. You gotta get screened"

forehead temperature check
and the questions of the day
"Have a cough?"
"Been around anyone sick?"

young pretty check-in lady
flirts with big male cop
in between screening the tired and huddled
he has a low baritone voice
she plays with her hair

more people come in the door of the emergency
room than leave through the door of the emergency
room
every third person requires a wheelchair
every sixth, a gurney

Chaplain in Hawaiian shirt walks out
carrying binder with title
'Counseling the Grieving'
tucked under left arm

"Ma'am. You gotta get screened"
a cop says

the vending machines only sell sugar free soda
as if sugar was the biggest thing
to worry about in an emergency room
at midnight
in Toledo

Militant Jesus

at first I laughed
when I heard someone say
that Trump was sent by God

but it stopped being funny
when I realized
they were serious

then
I watched
as cops and soldiers
terrorized Americans with tear gas

so Trump could take a picture
with a Bible
in front of a church

holding a holy book in the air
smiling
as Americans cried out

then I remembered
reading in scripture

that Jesus Wept

Dreamin' of Freedom

I know I should apologize
to someone
to everyone
but I won't

I'm on my 9th incarnation of this lifetime
and only a true bodhisattva
would double down
on getting a tenth chance

the candle blazes at both ends
because fire is the only thing that has ever loved me
I've went all in with so many lame hands in life
that satan herself
won't even sit at the poker table with me anymore

they keep putting whistleblowers in jail
while mafioso politicians play chess with human pawns
all the pandas are owned by the Chinese government
and I've decided I can no longer live in a world
where governments can own an entire protected
species

some people save money for their dreams
and some people dream in the noon sun
eyes wide open
racing into black holes

setting their hair on fire
so that the flames that consume them
will light a path for those
that dream
of freedom

From *One for Toledo Streets*

Foreword by Ben Stalets to the chapbook
One for Toledo Streets

It's the way that a nurse aboard an ambulance
doesn't bother to introduce themselves to the
girl curled up in the fetal position on the side of
the street. The way firefighters, back for a second
time in 15 minutes, having not taken the girl with
stomach pain seriously the first time, joke back and
forth about their beach volleyball game that night.
The way the sheriff passes carelessly in broad day
because it's only a black girl on the side of the
street suffering, not selling dope. It's the way that
even the people we pay to protect us can forget
that everyone needs to be treated like a person,
when they see someone without a home, living
in poverty. Those people are trained to deal with
situations like this. They're human and maybe all
nine of them had a bad day that time. Admittedly,
they certainly have a better handle on how to help
people than your average civilian. So, how bad do
you think this girl has been treated by your average
human, untrained, unaware?

There's a lot of people out there that spout
nonsensical, misinterpreted cliche's like "pick
yourself up by your bootstraps." Which is physically
impossible and misunderstands the sentiment the
author was making entirely. The only difference
between a person experiencing homelessness and
a person who isn't is just some wood and metal. Toledo

Streets Newspaper is wood and metal and
their mission is no holds barred employment,
community, change and hope.

You have a felony? Are you battling addiction? No
where else to turn? They're here for you. It's not
everything a person needs, but it's a group of people
who care and it's the start that's changed many lives.
Don't feel bad if you've never saw a need to help,
this is something our eyes have never been trained to
notice. But, once you see it, you can't unsee it.

Dan Denton is a special writer because he has dealt in
homelessness, addiction and mental illness. He's not
just empathetic, he knows. These poems humanize
many issues that are taboo in our lexicon. Dan is
caught somewhere between the metal and wood,
he's built a home and made a living for himself and
his family despite his years on the streets. He's a
published author, poet, union steward at Jeep, and
he's my friend.

The first time Dan (Denton) walked in to Toledo
Streets he began chatting with a couple vendors
immediately. I was worried he was going to be out of
touch, talk out of pocket. But when he started to talk,
the way they listened was unlike anything I've seen
before. I'll spare you the details, but I wouldn't be
writing this foreword if I didn't believe in his magic
and wisdom.

Words are just words when they only have ideas to inform them. Dan is more than just an idea, and these words are more than just poems. Toledo Streets is more than just a newspaper and the people they help are more than just homeless.

-Ben Stalets
Toledo Singer/Songwriter
Album Everyone's Laughing out everywhere

It's Not Squatting If You Leave
in the Morning

you can almost
lay out flat
in the backseat of an '85 Impala
and that's preferable
to trying to sleep on a park bench

but when they tow the Impala away
because it sat in the same spot
for over a month
it's ok to bundle up with two coats
in the corner of the living room
of an abandoned house

it'll still get cold in there
but a bottle of Thunderbird
will help you sleep

an old man named Charles
had been homeless for 15 years
and he knew things

"It's not squatting
if you leave in the morning,"
he told me,
"Cuz even baby Jesus
needed a stable to be born in."

I never figured out what
the infant Christ had to do with it
but I did make sure
me and my two coats
were always gone in the morning

Big Green Electrical Box
and East Rudy Dreams

when I was a kid
we used to play
on this big green electrical box
we tagged it with pink spray paint one summer
and another
I laid behind it
with an older girl
and after smoking a doobie
she gave me my first blow job

the big green electrical box
would come alive and hum
as ancient window fans
battled the summer heat

I think those electrical currents
got in our brains
and upset our rhythm
half of the group
that hung around the big green box
ended up hooked on drugs-
two of us never made it
out of those projects alive-
another died at 30
others
barely lived at all

I think about that girl sometimes
while I finger a 13 year sobriety chip
in the front pocket of my Levi's
did she ever find happy moments
or did she wind up drinking off-brand cola
with half-finished crossword puzzles
in week's old National Enquirers
sitting on a coffee table
in front of an old console television
blaring day-time game shows
just like her mother?

does she have kids?
a husband?
a job?
or is she still chasing East Rudy dreams
under rusty window fans
is she still riding a bike
down to the Community Market
that used to be a Wilb Walker's grocery store
30 years ago
when we were kids

is she stuck there
in Illinois
in the cornfields
two hours from the closest anything?

does the big green electrical box
still come alive

in the 600 block of East Rudy?
or has it been silenced
removed
forgotten
like a child's dreams
of rising above poverty?

The Cacophony of Human Life

somewhere
pedestrians wait for the traffic signal to change
truck drivers curse at motorists on the freeway
an ambulance howls weaving its way through traffic

somewhere
a junkie sticks a needle in her arm
a man stands on the railing of a bridge
a priest is slowly losing hope

somewhere
drunk people are falling in love at the corner bar
a bride walks slowly down an aisle
a funeral procession snakes it's way to the cemetery

a doctor prescribes a pill
an autoworker builds a car
a homeless man panhandles
a teacher grades papers
a cashier scans groceries
a stripper gets naked
an artist mixes paint

it's the song and dance of wasted human life
a cacophony of flatulence
that nestles into our ear canals
burrows into our brains
clings to our clothes

the song and dance of elevator music
of empty air
impotent ideas
sterile suggestions

the same old song and dance
the same yesterday
the same today
the same forever

The Icky Blues

those days
when you got
the icky blues

those days
when you got
a case of the sads
when you feel
just a little off

maybe you just didn't sleep well

maybe you forgot your meds
two days in a row

maybe Mercury is in retrograde

those days
when the blues are bluer
than just blue

when tying your shoes
feels like a week
with three Mondays

maybe it's just
one of those days

maybe it's nothing

or maybe it's not

Hair On Fire

work as many days as you can
take a day off
just before you have a stroke

sleep exactly half
the recommended hours needed

try to kick a pack a day habit
smoke a pack and a half tomorrow

forget to take your blood pressure pill
but only
once or twice a week

let your nagging morning blues
remind you
to call the doctor
then forget by lunch time

watch it all teeter
wonder if it'll fall

watch juggled balls bounce away
spinning plates smash on the floor

run til you almost crash
run til you crash

document the crash
do it again
do it again

hair on fire
dance
like there's no tomorrow

A Prayer for the Bipolar

mental debris
& bits of dignity
are strewn
up & down the block
just like
every other time
the bi-polar tornado roars through

pray to dead gods
that there's time to rebuild
before
the next storm arrives

& beg every god that
you can think of for mercy
that subsequent storm fronts
are weaker

Medicine for Busted Hearts

Thursday night in downtown Toledo
a blue collar town
built with brick and mud
built with work and blood

there's a bar
there's a patio
there's music

there's tall buildings crumbling to dust
concrete gardens and fading trust

there's a downtown skyline
and past that
there's neighborhoods and families
full of violence and drugs

out on the freeways that lead to different
Midwest towns with the same dead ends
there's human trafficking
and pollution of air and water
and pollution of human hearts

and past that
there's a thousand abandoned factories
that sit
like a thousand abandoned prayers

there's unemployment and homelessness
there's wars and droughts

there's kids with no mothers
and kids with no fathers
there's broken kids and there's hungry kids

there's desperation
sin and sadness
hate and confusion and madness

out there
past the patio
past the sounds of music and laughter
past the Thursday night blind dates
the cold beers
the jokes and the stories

out there
hope and happy
slip away
a little more each day

hope and happy
slip away
like factory 401k's
eaten by cancer

and it will all
still be

out there tomorrow
and out there next week and next month

but this Thursday night in downtown Toledo
the songwriters made rust belt poems
dance like daydreams that no one was watching
and guitars played
forgotten time-clock blues
that seep through
like medicine
like band aids and pain killers
for Toledo hearts
that are busted and bleeding
from all that out there

From the chapbook, C'mon Man Let's Talk About It, a book made to support a suicide awareness event in Toledo in 2022. 50 copies were printed and sold, helping raise over $300 for the Toledo chapter of National Alliance of Mental Illness (NAMI.)

C'mon Man Let's Talk About It

this one goes out to the men
kings and warriors
my brothers

don't you think
it's time to talk about it
how we account for
76% of all suicides in America?

look I get it
we're tough
we're strong
we're all bend and no break
we are real men don't cry

look brother I get it
we're don't ask for help with something
we can do ourselves
we're stand tall
we don't talk about it- we be about it

I get it but I don't care
not when we
lose 99 American men everyday
not when suicide
is the third leading cause
of death among 15-24 year olds

yo let's talk about it
about how maybe man up means to speak up
before there's another
man down

about how you can't stand tall
when you're no longer standing
how you can't be there
when you're no longer here

let's talk about it
about how we've already lost too many
fathers and brothers friends and sons

let's talk about it
about how there's dynamics
that come with masculinity
that we don't understand-
but they might kill us

let's talk about it
and talk about it
until it's no longer taboo to ask for help
until we make it ok
for men to feel vulnerable

let's talk about it
until the last man standing knows
he never stood alone
c'mon man let's talk about it

White Knuckle Sunrise

when you're rocking
in your kitchen chair at 3am
having a sleepless stare down
with a cup of black coffee

when your walls echo
with a thousand whispers
and haunts sit in your restless lap

when your thoughts go quiet
and you're left
with the small talk
of a ticking clock

when nothing moves but the jump
in your jittery legs
when your room seems too big
and too small all at once
and you're alone
counting absentminded heartbeats
instead of sheep

so alone that minutes crawl
like slow death and silence rings
in your ears
like a telephone
that you can't answer

hold steady
dig deep
find your reason why
and hug it
like your life depends on it

and wait for the safety
that comes
with another
white knuckle sunrise

My Heart is a Ghost Town

I drive down highways of the hopeful
with my windows up
and my hollow ears watch
life drive by around me

work shifts come and go
bills come and keep coming
each hour counts another bygone
I confuse my prayers for daydreams

my heart is a ghost town
my candle a footnote
the bygones melt into moments
that stretch ahead forever
like nothing
like empty
like clouds with no rain

Remember When

remember the soft orange smile of a spring sunset

remember the clear blue forever of July skies

remember the first kisses that meant something

remember the ones that said thank you

remember the ones that said you're welcome

remember the most beautiful sunrise you've ever seen

remember all the times that the moon took your
breath away

remember the hugs of your children

remember the hugs your children gave that you didn't
ask for

remember that the jokes about being bipolar will only
last so long and you'll live alone with the stigmas

when the depression gains hold of your heart
and the hours bloom like car crashes

when you stop finding rainbows after the rain
and hope seems like a laughing matter
when the hurt becomes an aching shadow
and life loses it's flavor

remember that spring always follows winter and that
death isn't always forever

Sometimes I Hate This Fucking Life

because I keep reading headlines
about train passengers videotaping a rape
instead of calling the cops
but I'm too much of a coward
to click the links & read the story

because I know a dozen people that are struggling
& I don't know the words to tell them to make it ok
because I'm struggling, too
& I don't know how to tell anyone
how do you tell someone that's suicidal
that you've been feeling real what's the point, too?

because my friends are hurting
& I don't know the words to make it ok
because my friends are hurting themselves
& I don't know the words to make it ok
because my friends are hurting & they don't deserve
the hurt

because Portsmouth Ohio is Portsmouth Ohio
& Toledo is Toledo

because the American healthcare system is the
American healthcare system

because American hurt is American hurt
& I don't know the words to make it ok

because Americans are hurting
& hurting themselves
& I don't know the words to make it ok

sometimes I hate this fucking life
because we are all hurting
& I don't know how to make it ok

Anxiety Eats a Wooden Heart

anxiety eats at my wooden heart
like termites
turning a home to dust

it's October—
the gray fall
& its morning chill
sprinkle depression in my oatmeal

too many days
of factory work in a row
has wiped away
the last
of last month's sunshine

the shadows of my neighbors
block any remaining light
from my doorways & windows
my eyes fumble to see

the anxiety
& the termites
continue
to eat in the dark

This is Depression

the sky is gray
every hour is gray
your heart is gray
& sex
isn't sex anymore
porn isn't porn
just food that feeds
the gray hours

a heartbeat is just a zig zag line
on a chart in a folder
in some doctor's file cabinet

nothing is nothing
& everything is nothing
the days are nothing
the minutes are agonizing in their nothingness

the horizon is nothing
& there is nothing
forever
as far as you can see

sleep isn't sleep
it's time spent
between feeling nothing & nothing

food isn't food
your fork isn't a fork
it's an extension of the nothing

knives are still knives
but they cut nothing

& the nothing is crushing
consuming

until finally you are nothing
& I am nothing
& I feel nothing
& I know nothing but nothing

See What Happens Next

the feelings of unease
settle all around like a soaking mist
the hands of despair and nothing
claw at my throat
I push through for as long as I can
for hours and days and weeks
until the nothing starts to fill up my lungs
and I choke on every breath

I think of the rafters in my old garage
wondering if they could hold my weight
if I tied a rope around one of them
I wonder if I should write a note
or call 911 right before I step off the chair
so that the emergency personnel will find me
and my friends won't have to live out their days
with the image of me hanging lifeless
imprinted in the forefront of their morning thoughts
the way some of my friends have left me

I think of all the summers that I've lived through
Summer my favorite season
when the days are long with sunshine and heat
and the nights are short and easy to sleep through
it's my 39th summer and I've yet to see it all

there are manuscripts started
and piled up under a shelf in my basement
dozens of them

and I think about finishing one
or five or ten
and I wonder if anyone would publish them
and who would read them

and those 13 states that I've yet to visit
how are the people there?
do they have museums filled with the magic
of yesterday's art?

and my children
what will they grow to be?
how long will it take them to learn
the important things in life—
the things that I've tried and failed
to show them—
will they struggle to find escapes too?

there's too much that I've yet to see
and there's too many words that I've yet to write

I gotta shoulder on through another hour
another day
another week
just to see what happens next

Like a Badge of Honor

I have to swipe my 9 year old work badge
11 times every morning
before it'll let me in to work
and I could trade it for a new one
but it has my first day photo on it
and I know a guy in the factory
that's had the same photo for 46 years—
he wears his work badge like a badge of honor

it's like an aching back
from a long day's work

like a proud dent on the fender
of a humble pick up truck

like a half moon
neither full nor empty

this badge of honor that I've carried
in three different wallets
that were not made for the factory life

I think I'll keep it
as long as it still
let's me in to a place
that I often joke
is ran by a warden

maybe it's like how we
wear our smiles
like scars of survival

or like a hug from a sad friend
that makes you happy

Andy My Friend

I'll always remember sitting on the front porch
when we were in the halfway house together
we'd chain-smoke cigarettes
and talk about art and history
trying to ignore the reality
of how our addictions had beat us down
and how our mental illnesses were always
trying to finish us off

I'll always remember the times we had coffee
we'd take the bus and order $5 drinks
and pretend like we fit in
with the yuppies drinking their soy lattes
we both knew we didn't belong there
but we tried
because the coffee shop was better
than the gutters we'd climbed out of

I bought that piece of art from you
because I loved it
and you needed money to buy
some groceries and a gift for
your Mother on Mother's Day
it's proudly displayed in the living room
five years later

Andy my friend
I'm not mad that you jumped or that you're gone
I can't be mad at the ones that have helped me
get through my own madness

Andy, my friend
whatever the afterlife looks like
I hope the addictions and mental illnesses
are gone
and I hope you're at peace

Andy my friend
don't worry about us back here
we'll struggle along just fine
and I'll look at your art
now and again
and be grateful
that I'm still here to remember

From *Junkyard Heart*
(The Lunch Bucket Brigade, 2025.)

...and it's only fucking Wednesday

worked
fingers to bone
bone to dust

lived a dozen sleepless nights

tried to rescue
a host of guardian angels & failed

started 10 diets
gained 2 pounds
fought & lost
100 wars

crashed a dozen times
on dirt trails
of heartbreak & madness

burned through all of
yesterday's bridges

and it's only fucking Wednesday man

and it's only fucking Wednesday

How to Make it Through December

turn the thermostat up to a tropical 74 degrees
fuck the gas company & their monthly bill

eat the holiday cookies
eat all the holiday cookies
fuck calories
they don't matter

spend too much on presents
spend more than you have
fuck credit
it's make believe anyway

if you drink - drink more
if you smoke- get lost in clouds
if you don't smoke or drink
pray

lust after comfort
warmth & love

honor the old standards
hug yourself in security blanket embrace
wear pajamas for 3 days
or wear nothing at all

fornicate with yourself
but only if it's consensual
watch reindeer porn just to feel something

give in to the hopelessness
let the half empty glass
drain all the way

It's a January Day

it's the removing
of a fresh blanket
of new snow
every morning

the careful way
you pluck
the windshield wipers
letting them fall
three times
against the glass

it's the tires
always leaking air
in January
as if tire air
migrates to Florida
for the winter

it's the 24 years
of kicking snow clumps
off already
too heavy
work boots

the 24 years
of doing two days

worth of work
every day
it's a life
of only making enough
to get by
a week at a time

it's an aging pick up truck
with arthritic brakes
and an engine
in desperate need
of a massage

it's a tiredness
that rides shotgun
across
uneven railroad tracks
down
sleeping streets
into
ice cold factories

where machines growl
before you've even
had time
to warm up

The Gray March

it was one of those gray March days
one where it rains off and on and it's cold
but not cold enough to snow

the air all around you seems dead
and people are reflecting deadness in their eyes
the clocks are moving eight minutes slow every hour
so the entire business of living through this one day
takes three hours longer than it should

the trees are still standing like skeletons from
summers past

these are the days that are made for whiskey and soup
I don't know how many more of these
that I can live through
I've lived through so many already
that the extra three hours have piled into
an extra three years
though the social security administration
refuses to acknowledge it

Friday Night Sirens

there's always something
about a payday pocket fat with hope
that drives a man to chasing

full moons
in midnight
dive bars

chasing
higher highs
lower lows

chasing
Friday night sirens
in too short skirts
with too thick thighs

chasing
comfort
in bottles & syringes

comfort
in the arms of
& between the legs of
trains
waiting to be derailed

chasing
powder keg lovers
that go together
like cornbread & grease

sweet on Friday nights
full of heartburn
on Saturday mornings

Summer Nights

I live for summer nights
when the bugs swarm street lamps
and the inner city hookers
walk with swagger

the summer nights that last forever
when you sit outside under midnight moons
with your quirky friends
watching a fire burn low
laughing until the dawn breaks

when neighborhoods come alive
as the sun goes down and the heat fades
over house parties and backyard s'mores

these are the nights that live forever in the hearts
of men
when police sirens wail and motorcycles roar
random fireworks displays break out
and you give no fucks about early morning work
days

yeah man
I live for summer nights
nights made for lovers
sleeping naked in tangled sheets
as the air conditioner in the window
hums a lullaby

nights full of endless hope and camaraderie
of sin and lust
when we're all immortal
if even just
for the season

Midnight Virus

at the midnight hour
lonely people
lie awake
in big soft beds
windows open
the summer heat
heavy in the air
slowly choking
them to sleep

frazzled men
with two day beards
sit at the counters of local diners
drinking bitter coffee
while their death clocks
tick away

at the midnight hour
rodents come alive under the street lights
roaming empty streets
feasting on garbage
whores hustle the next trick
dealers make a late run
ghosts dance in the open
children lie in tender sleep
a mother's prayers rise
like steam from a kettle

sadness seeps through the walls
at the midnight hour
those infected with midnight virus
shuffle and hustle
passion plea prayers to a thousand gods
with statue ears
that only echo
but never hear

Guts

the sidewalks will laugh at you
as rough cement
tears through denim
and scrapes smooth skin
from your knee

the trees will whisper into the breeze
thinking that you
have lost your way

the sun will hide her face
darkening your worst moments

the clouds will open
and rain on you
or close themselves off
and leave you
high and dry

the grass is uncaring

the gods may smirk at your misfortunes
but they don't know
the stuff
that you are made of

they don't know
why you force yourself
to awaken
and face each day

none of this matters -
not the bloody knees
not the bruised ego -
the rumors are irrelevant
darkness can not swallow your fire
rainy days and droughts are rarely fatal

all that matters
is if you have the guts
to keep on going

the gods know nothing about guts
do you?

Lucky

*"If it wasn't for bad luck, I wouldn't
have no luck at all"*

-lyrics by soul singer William Bell

No luck
Bad luck
Tough luck

Good luck
Fuck luck
Make your own luck

Lottery luck
Raffle ticket luck
Dumb luck

Some people
have all the luck
Some
don't even know
what luck is

Still Life With Gouda

while eating
smoked Gouda
& grapes
I like to set
each bite
to the sweet
of the grape
hitting
the tongue first
followed
by the salt
of the cheese
fighting
it's way forward

sweet
like dreams
salt
like truth

like
those tears
I could
have cried
but didn't

sweet grape
salt truth

turns out
it only
mattered
to me

Junkyard Heart

every backyard mechanic
knows
that the cheapest way
to keep
an old car running
is to go
out to the edge of town
to an old junkyard
where
you can pull
your own used parts

but what
am I to do
about
my own crumbling
infrastructure

what am I to do
with these knees
turning to dust
these knuckles on my hands
that are twice as big
as their younger selves
these feet
battered & beaten
by factory floors

& this heart
that's long overdue
for a tune-up

this heart
that's been left set
to full open throttle
for too long

this heart
that's been broken
& repaired so many times
that even duct tape
ain't working
to hold it together
anymore

where is the junkyard
that will take
these old bones
as trade
for still working parts

where is the junkyard
where I can go pull
my own
used heart

From *Hope is a Lost Dog*
(The Lunch Bucket Brigade, 2023.)

One For National Poetry Month

America
pays for her sins
by throwing months away
to the things that capitalism
does not have time to care about

that's not a political statement
just an observation

think about it
breast cancer awareness
suicide prevention
mental health awareness

you can see where this is going
are there more and better clinics for cancer?
are suicide rates declining?

it's too saddening to start on
Women's History Month
and my heart breaks for African-Americans
and how hard the fight has been
to find history
in this white washed system

I know poetry month
should mean something
but what?

when all the poets I know
die in obscurity?

alas
the government and the people
and the poets
keep sucking me back in

not because I think
that this poetry month
will turn the tide

it's because poetry
has always been
the only spark left
when things go dark
in my heart

Fire in My City

there's a fire up ahead
somewhere in the city
it's always hard to tell with fire
or any disaster
they could be
a dozen miles away
or just beyond
the next neighborhood

there's a fire this morning
in my city
you can see the smoke billow
like a black
mile high geyser
it towers over
the payday loan places
and the junkyards
where working people
watch their futures
get crushed beneath mountains
of rust and debt

there's a fire this morning
in my city
where the fire trucks bounce and dodge
west Toledo potholes
and wrestle their way

through kamikaze intersections
where religion rides
on rusty-clunker bumper stickers

there's a fire this morning
in my city
you can see the smoke
rise over
the buy here- pay here car lots
that live on every corner
of every neighborhood
where hourly wages
go to drown
in pools of inflation

there's a fire
in my city
burning over the metro park trees
and old buildings
with wrinkled faces
that have held Toledo dreams
for too many
industrial stagnations

there's a fire in my city
up ahead
where the next
disaster
waits to rip
and tear

through my neighborhood
that has already
suffered enough

there's a fire
in west Toledo
where the firemen and women
race my working neighbors
to hell
and struggle
to get there first
just like
every other Wednesday

Stray Dog Smile

went down
to the city pound
to register
my pooch
for another year

sat in the parking lot
and watched
as stray dogs
played
in outdoor kennels

splashing in kiddie pools
chasing tails
and chewing toys

a dozen Toledoans
lined up to laugh
and chase
stray dog smiles

chasing proof
that there's still
joy
inside the kennels
we're all
forced to play in

Can't Afford to Cry

I'm from a cliche generation
from a cliche small Midwestern town
where they did indeed
brainwash us
with cliche'd public educations
that taught us
that boys don't cry

like everything else
like the thanksgiving story and the constitution
like America is a free country
full of checks and balances
I found that boys don't cry
is another
big lie

until 30
I only cried
when anger ripped
through my heart and tore my lungs
but since then
I've cried
a little more each year

I learned
that happy tears are the same
as sad ones

but they taste better
when you choke them
behind
a tough guy facade

I learned
that sunglasses help a poker face
especially
when the stakes
are worth more than money

I learned
that America is a lie
that boys do cry-
and a tough guy
might leak tears
during mental breakdowns
or at the funeral
for another friend
strangled by addiction

I learned
that tears
can give strength
and bring laughter
and they sure can heal
and wash
a dirty heart

Hope is a Lost Dog

the flowers have been left
unwatered
and alone
for too long
if weeding
was a war
I've already lost
in this incarnation
and the next

I see clowns juggling sin
in the morning parade down brain street
a mariachi band
marches ahead of tomorrow's elevator music

whirligigs and firecracker explosions
live two and three houses over
church bells ring a day late
radio static crackles from city sidewalks

hope is a lost dog looking for home
pickpockets steal money
from the hearts of naked men
restless nights are
a foregone conclusion
forever is a car crash
every afternoon
at the same intersection

Sunday Sermon on the River

when my heart gets empty
from being squeezed
like a dirty dishrag
I like to go
down to the River
to pray

Summer Sunday afternoon
and the wildflowers
nobody planted
lent their fragrance-
incense for the holy
and unwanted

red-winged blackbirds
chirped a choir chorus
I sat on a bench
to watch the boats
as the clouds smiled
across the River top
and water roared by

and soon enough
my wrung naked heart
opened
and began to sing along

Rip the Bandaid Off

when you live
a mosh pit
blue collar life
full
of trailer park love and back alley slam dances
you're gonna
get hurt
sometimes

I've always
believed
in ripping
the bandaid off
no sense
in avoiding
discomfort

pop the pimples
probe the scars
poke around the infections
in your heart with punk rock lyrics
squeeze the cysts
howl with the hurt
run with the wolves
and never appear
as prey

look for healing
alone
and under
empty night skies
the stars
know more than they're telling
but you've got
to learn to listen

find the salve
in nature
hug trees
and kiss bees
dance amongst
the briars
damn the arm hair
and the tender skin
on the bottom of your eyelids
rip the fucking bandaid loose
scream and cuss
if you must

only the living bleed
and pain
is nothing
but a prayer
for comfort

Namaste Motherfucker

wake up for work
take time to meditate
to find peace in the morning
Namaste

traffic is slow
through the construction zone
but you left early enough
Namaste

the supervisor is yelling
because the line is stopped
but you smile and shrug it off
Namaste

two coworkers laugh
at a homophobic slur
you grit your teeth
politely tell them it's offensive
they call you a faggot lover
Nam-as-te

hour nine of a ten hour shift
and you're grinding
to just make it
through a long day
N-a-m-a-s-t-e

a truck honks at you
because you're driving
too slow on the way home
the truck swerves erratically
pausing alongside you to yell and cuss
and give you the finger
you take a deep meditative breath
FUCK YOU!
Namaste motherfucker
Namaste

From *Love Song for Toledo,*
(The Lunch Bucket Brigade, 2023)

Love Song for Toledo

Toledo my city
it's been 20 years now
since I've called you home
20 years with
your backward politics
and troublesome gun violence

Toledo I've learned to love you
and you
were the first city
to love me back

Toledo you lose
and gain manufacturing jobs
like a bipolar Wall Street ticker
your streets are forever crumbling
and half the restaurants and businesses
are boarded up
like buildings that
are waiting for a windfall storm that never comes

Toledo you average sized city
with a big city chip on your shoulder
you silly city you
that takes advantage of good traffic
by never learning how to drive
that gives downtown riverfront property away

to a poorly managed
hospital system that takes back its promises
Toledo you silly city
that barely has a newspaper
and can't figure out
how to entertain
or retain its youth

Toledo you have been home
to so many artists
but when will you finally learn how to love?
you put our art on the sidewalks -
buildings and bridges and silos -
when will you let us put our art
in your heart?
when will you learn?
to cater to us?
instead of the rich LPGA sponsors
that visit once a year
then treat us like an afterthought?
when will you give us tax breaks
instead of the big factories
that are forever threatening to leave you?

Toledo you beautiful city
I first met you when I lived
in the old dirty south end
I was drinking then
and writing love songs to dive bars
on South Ave and Arlington

dive bars on Western Ave
and South Broadway

Toledo I got sober with you
in your old North End
where hope is not sold in the corner store
Toledo I've lived in your snooty suburbs
until I found home
next to the giant junkyards and sprawling factories
of working West Toledo
all of my neighbors have one
or two or three jobs
to keep up on our auto insurance
and outrageous fucking Buckeye Cable bills
all of my neighbors work and eat here
and grow rust in their spines
to show they're from Toledo
it's a Toledo thing
like Jeep and Mudhens
you'd have to live here to understand

Toledo I love you
but I see my neighbors you've forgotten
like Doug the alcoholic with cancer
who stands invisible
holding a cardboard sign
dying in ways no one ever sees
like my neighbor Maureen
that retired from two jobs at 70
and drinks two bottles of $7 vodka a day

I have to help her take down
the Easter decorations
here in our West Toledo slum lord apartments
who else will help her?
not you Toledo
who keeps forgetting her artists
if we let you

Toledo my beautiful adopted city
where I have found a sober life
and a union job
where I have grown into a man
that likes to think he's kind
although there are some
like the customer service rep
from the power company that I talked to last week
who do not say kind things about me

Toledo you average city
with a big city attitude and big city problems
you average city
with a big city art scene
with big city talent and diversity
Toledo there are 100 artists
that try to love you everyday
but haven't I given you
more love poems than the rest?
haven't I carried your chip
on my shoulder
and your blue collar grit in my heart

Toledo I sang your praises
in a dozen cities last year
in Detroit and Nashville and Chicago
in Dearborn and Michigan City
reading and roaring poems
from Jersey and NYC to Illinois and Wisconsin
but you never call me an ambassador
I do it for free
I do it for love

Toledo it's been 20 years
and you were the first city
to call me an artist
some people say
that I'm your artist
that I'm the best writer in Toledo
that I'm the Bukowski of Toledo
they say I am Toledo
and in some places
in some small circles
when they hear Dan Denton
they think of Toledo

Toledo I've learned to love you
warts and hemorrhoids and all
Toledo my city
I come alive
dancing down your dangerous freeways
singing hymns to your working class
on avenues
broken and damned

Toledo let's do better here
Toledo we've both got so much potential
Toledo tell me you love me
as sirens rain down W. Alexis Rd again tonight
Toledo slow dance with me at dawn
to our patron Saint of the Arts -
the great Art Tatum-
who you have practically ignored

Toledo I have loved with all that I am
and here I stand alone again
drugs and violence and poverty
stretching from here to City Hall

the spring sun is struggling to rise
and it is gray and 45 degrees
for the 10th day in a row

Thursday Night in Toledo

coffee gurgles and drips in the coffee pot
the cat scratches in his litter box
three days worth of unopened mail
sits tall on the table
leaning against a pile of books
I sometimes can't see over

spark an after work joint
check the bank account
there's $2.99
the day before payday
it's a frozen Banquet dinner
alone
and with a plastic fork
again tonight

two cigarettes
and a cup of coffee
for dessert

Friday Night in Toledo

Friday night
finally payday
and a trip to the dispensary
the bank account is flush

a nap after
a long factory shift
and before
the weekly jaunt
to the grocery store
one of the ones
staffed by union workers

most of the bills are paid
I got two scratch off tickets
and a $5 cigar
and still
a little jangle
in the pocket
of my good Levi's

it's Friday night
in Toledo
it's fried egg sandwiches
and William Carlos Williams poems

a cup of coffee
with late night daydreams
and the yawning possibilities
that come
with a weekend off
from the factory

Let Them Eat Bullets

the day after another school shooting
and I go for
my daily walk
in my midwestern city
that's messy
and full of potholes
and division
just like every where else

music plays in my earbuds
Wu Tang Clan
urges me
to bring the motherfuckin' ruckus
it has been one hour
since the most recent spring thunderstorm
blew through
I walk along a busy
five lane road
there's mud on the sidewalk
and in my heart

all around me
I'm surrounded
by poverty and inflation
peeling billboards and rust
genders are debated
by folks that have never

had to debate with themselves
over their own gender
dead brown crab grass
grows in the parking lots
of dozens of abandoned businesses
along my route

I feel a collective cry
and the only answer
our American politicians
can bring us so far is
to let us peasants
eat bullets

Late on a Toledo February Night

sometimes
late on a Toledo February night
when the cold and the dark
stare back at us
like reflections of ourselves
through bedroom windows
that were never meant
to serve as mirrors

sometimes
late on a Toledo February night
when the winter wind
rattles your bones
until your will corrodes
the factory hours pile up on a man
and all life's bad decisions
laugh in the background at once

sometimes
late on a Toledo February night
your lungs begin to recall
every cigarette lit and scoffed at
and the arthritis in your hip
and shoulder
and both knees
all come to collect
their rent at the same time

sometimes
late on a Toledo February night
your every heartbeat
will recall every heartbreak
and heart hurt
and heart punch
your heart has known
and your unopened mail
will remind you
that your body still bears scars
you might never
be able to pay for

Rusty Snow Bones

I worked a 10 hour factory shift
just like any other Monday
rushed home
fed the cat
made the coffee
and showered away
rustbelt blues

took the coffee to go
hurried up
when I should be winding down
and headed out the door
to see my head-shrinker therapist

it was the middle of March
and the gray sky
laughed with impunity

a snow squall
snuck in on 5pm traffic
and everyone slowed
like we had blue cards
hanging from rear view mirrors
as all of our cars
remembered to waddle like ducks
when walking on ice

and I snapped -
a full on cosmic breakdown
I gripped the steering wheel
like a man
that's just trying to hang on
and I yelled and screamed
and I called Mother Nature
all of the worst combined insults
that I've ever yelled at anyone

for fuck's sake
a man's bones
can only handle
so much Monday
can only handle
so much snow and gray

a man's bones
can only bear the weight
of so many stoplights
and potholes
so many LED billboards
and half empty strip malls

a man's bones
ain't made to see
a bundled up panhandler
standing in a snow cyclone
praying for a snowball's chance in hell
to get a dollar

fuck you Mother Nature
and life
and all the gods
old and new
real and fake
fuck you
fuck you
fuck you

The Neighborhood
My Family Calls Home

there's a dollar store
a hippie head shed
two cell phone stores
a payday loan place
a pawn shop

there's two bars
a gas station
a paint store

there's four parts places
for four different
types of industry

there's a hardware store
a grocery store
& a pet store

there's a used tire shop
and a colossal junkyard
for smashed up cars

there's a bank for your dollars
a vet for your pets
& a church for your soul

there's a dozen empty buildings
offices & store fronts

down on Lewis Ave.
between Laskey & Alexis

where there's potholes & rust
& driveways with cars that cuss

where all the parks
are full of weeds & sick trees

where there's GEDs
& scratch off ticket dreams

down on Lewis Ave.
between Laskey & Alexis
the neighborhood
that my family
calls home

Part II

on the other side of the tracks
where the Mayor lives
there's nothing
but big houses
with big yards
& big garages
with big cars

there's parks
full of sunshine & sparkling water
there's dreams growing on boulevards

where there's hope in every mailbox
& the college degrees grow on trees

where the Mayor lives
the streets are shiny & new
& all the stoplights have happy faces

where the mayor lives
there's no box stores
or small business
just neighborhoods
& houses
& people that might have problems
but you don't see them
out on the street
like you do
on Lewis Ave.
between Laskey & Alexis
the neighborhood my family calls home

Other Selected Work

At the Holland Haus

at the Holland Haus
a one car garage music venue
listening to local bands jam
I found the heart I lost
when I was 27

crowded in there
shoulder to shoulder
with music filling in
any space leftover

lead singers
giving it everything they had
for 50 people
on a random Saturday night

I felt the rhythm
vibrating in my bones
my feet tapping
involuntary beats

out there at Holland Haus
on the edge of Toledo
but right square
in the middle of
all this heart

Fight Song for the Underdog

this is for every human
that's ever lived with depression-
for every human
that's ever lived
with a voice inside their head
that keeps whispering
"Kill. Kill. Kill yourself."

this is for all the big folks
standing in line at McDonald's
ordering a salad and a Diet Coke

this is for all the pimply faced teenaged boys
walking down high school hallways
trying to work up the courage to say 'hi'
to a cheerleader

this is a fight song

this is for all the poor kids
that are thumbing through
Car & Driver magazine
daydreaming about Lamborghinis

this is for every little girl that's ever
dreamed of growing up to be a princess
and whose parents could never afford
to even buy Barbie's plastic dream house

this is an anthem
this is for all the geeks that have ever played chess
this is for all the cover band lead singers
wailing their lungs out at the empty corner bar
this is for all the old men
walking to the carry out
to play their pick 3 numbers
and to buy a pack of one dollar cigars for the day

this is your fight song

this is for you and for me
for everyone that's ever felt invisible
and unloved and less than
this is for everyone that's ever felt fat
or too thin and especially
for the ones that have ever been told those things
and for everyone that's ever wished that their tits
were bigger
or that their dick was bigger
or wished that they had just one friend

this is for anyone that's ever been laid off
fired from work
or dumped
for anyone that's ever been alone
on Thanksgiving or at Christmas time

this is the day the comeback probably doesn't happen
but you hang on anyway

this is for all the queers
that have ever had to live life
pretending that they weren't
for any reason

this is for the weirdos and the nerds
the misfits and the dragon slayer book readers
the gamers and the wizards
the witches and the furries too

this is a fight song for those excluded
because they just didn't fit in
despite having flower gardens for hearts

this is for the guy working a low wage job
standing at the bus stop every morning
in subzero temperatures
counting down the days until Friday
because he's out of smokes
and his lights are about to get shut off
and he hasn't had anything to eat except soup
for the last three days
this is for the ones that have no idea how they're
going to make it through the winter months
this is for the ones that are forever hanging on by
a thread
this is for the ones too poor to file for bankruptcy
this is for for the ones
that get up and go to work everyday anyway
and for the ones that get up

and go to work everyday until they can't
because
god -damn -it
this is for the underdogs

this is our fucking fight song

It's All Over (part 1)

I've gone and done it now
burned up
the last of my brain power
I've been living
off the reserves for years
but it's all over now

it happened after one too many
dead dick days
in a brain dead factory
I've squinted my eyes
and gritted my teeth
against the mundane
for too long
but it's all over now

how much do you expect one man to endure?
37 years 10 months and 25 days is it
I've got biscuits for brains now

it's all gonna be ok
I can take my rightful place
in this dead dick world
eating Cheetos
and watching
the same old tired reruns
on cable television

I can hang up my ballpoints
put the notebooks
in the kitchen's junk drawer
I can rest easy
I fought the good fight for so long
but it's all over now

Maybe it ain't over yet (part 2)

when you're dry
bone dry
lips cracked and scaling over dry
it only takes a tiny spark
to start a roaring fire

I rustle around all day
hunting that spark
listening to gray noises
reading gray words

I've chewed on so many thoughts and ideas
that the roof of my mouth is raw
none of them hit the spot

I just need that one idea
I know I'm just one spark
one good poem away
from being consumed by the fire

The Summer of No Parades

remember that one summer
when time stood still
when we all got lost and confused
kept waking up in ghost towns

that one summer when not one American
bought a single ticket
to a single baseball game
when America's past time
became an afterthought

remember when we all gave up
on any summer concerts
when we all stayed home
when going to the park almost
felt like freedom

remember when health officials became
more important than politicians
for a moment
before corporate America
wrestled back the remote control
and returned us to the regularly scheduled
programming

remember when average Americans
stricken with cabin fever

stumbled into the streets
and marched into the teeth
of chemical weapons
and fascism

remember the summer when capitalism
killed all the parades
emptied downtown streets of joy
and communion
when celebrations became nearly extinct

remember the summer when grocery store clerks
and nurses and doctors
and grocery getter providers
became more important than cops
and soldiers and celebrities

remember when the world turned on its side
for a year
when hope was nearly thrown off it's axis

remember when we stood
at yet another turning point
wondering if this time
we had the energy
to fight on

Sunday Mornings

Sunday mornings
the only mornings
work doesn't call me out of bed at 4am
the only morning
we can spend together
bodies curled into and wrapped
around the other

and as happens with lovers
clothes come off
and it's skin on skin
lips on collar bones
fingers pulling hair
cock and cunt
whispers and laughs
thrusts and moans

then it's off to the kitchen
to soft music
to lit cigarettes
to smells of coffee
and frying bacon
conversations and
reflections
of another week together

and then breakfast-
toast in egg yolk
fried potatoes
seasoned with pepper
that crisp bacon
and the trusty sidekick of
a favorite mug
full of strong
hot coffee

then it's soft chairs
more cigarettes and more coffee
books and comfort
and love

later it's football
then naps

it's sunday in Walbridge, OH
a holy day in
every factory town of America

A Coltrane Night

I just want to sit
read
& listen to Coltrane

bent horn blue notes
drifting down
empty Tuesday night streets
where all the working families
have tucked their kids to bed
read stories
& kissed foreheads

where factory fathers have
drank the last of
their 4th longneck
as the family dog
sniffs the perimeter of
a backyard
with a dimmer switch
set to January clear
starry night

Coltrane
like ice water
spiking lightening
in brain freeze
11pm hearts

Coltrane
setting down
an exclamation point
with a silk blanket thud

Long Live the Ink Pen

I will not post pictures of the French flag
on social media
what use is a flag
when monsters
are amongst us?

I will not pray for the victims
what use is prayer
when the terrorists pray too?

what use is a god
when those that kill
and those that kill in return
do so
in the name of god?

no
I will not try to comfort myself
or others
with nonsense

instead
I will allow the sorrow
to seep into my bones
and the hopelessness
to wash me away

to where?
to here
carry me away
to my safe place
to paper, and pen

the pen might not be mightier
than the sword
but words have lived long enough
to watch most every
god fall from grace

imagine a world where people
believed in people
and left the gods to fight over
whether they believed
in themselves

Two Hot Dogs On A Paper Plate

the alarm clock
has no empathy
for a man
that's working two jobs

10 hours in a factory
that manufactures
a get by
a week at a time
paycheck

four more hours
in a gig economy
plus two styrofoam cups
of gas station coffee

& the chatter of the world
rattles like the wind
through a rusty chime

the cops
murdered
another black man

a mass shooting
the third
this week

politicians
do politician things
the news
is the news

America
is the same
but different
& dinner
is two hot dogs
on a paper plate

Everything is Coronavirus

The grass in my yard has coronavirus
The flowers in the vase on my table have coronavirus
My dog has coronavirus
The green grapes in the green strainer on my
kitchen counter have coronavirus

The mailman has coronavirus
The morning news and the evening news both have
coronavirus
My television has coronavirus
If I still had a radio it would have coronavirus

My unread books have coronavirus
My cigarettes have coronavirus
My vitamin D pills that I take in the morning have
coronavirus
My hair has coronavirus

My neighbor has coronavirus
Your neighbor has coronavirus

The gas station clerk, the school crossing guard,
and the babe that pulls the winning lottery ping
pong balls just before midnight, all have coronavirus

This poem probably has coronavirus
But it can't get a test til Tuesday
and the hospitals are already full

Jelly Donuts Suck

woke up on a Saturday
feeling like a guy
that hasn't had a good dream
in a year

my morning routine
did not include
packing any motivation
& I forgot my lunch
at home

frost covered Toledo
like the wrong kind of blanket
& my feet were cold
all the way to work

the sun came up
& made the yellow leaves
on the autumn trees
come alive

we had donuts at work
because it was Saturday
so I ate a jelly donut
because I hate jelly donuts

The Factory Bells & Whistles

the factory whistles blow early
calling work worn & weary bodies
out of
it ain't even fucking dawn yet beds

tired & sleeping feet
with soles roughened
by 20 fucking years
of heartless concrete factory floors,
jammed into overworked & under-appreciated
work boots
that are 9 weeks past
their expiration date

Christmas bells jingle in late November
like an ever growing crescendo
all the factory dads and moms
add & re-add the remaining
available overtime hours
and repeat a maybe if I don't-take-no-more -
days-off til Christmas mantra

behind all the factory bells and whistles
the working class sends smoke signaled & socially
distanced holiday wish lists
to a not yet seen this year Santa
a hell, maybe he's quarantined Santa

a don't you think someone should check on him
Santa

tell him
we only want
a weekend off
and the means to production
so that there'll finally be world peace
out on the factory floor

Lottery Dreams

a dark dirt road
a single wide trailer
with a single strand
of struggling Christmas lights

the hollow bark
of a brown dog
in a fenced yard
the terror
of a fuel light
blinking
on the freeway
with 20 miles to go

a growling stomach
two crumpled one dollar bills
in a frayed blue jean pocket
the taste of bologna with no cheese
an old tire that needs air every morning

having the right to an attorney
is never the same as having one
we all have lottery ticket dreams
but some tickets
mean more to others

there are many places
that an empty stocking
is hung with more care
than a full one

Don't Let Your Puppies Grow Up to be K-9 Cops

because no one likes a snitch
even if it's a pooch

get 'em hooked on Milk Bones
and let 'em roam the local alleys
looking for stray bitches

take them for walks
but don't instill too much discipline
because that's kind of overdone
and really
the best doggos are free spirits
and free spirited canines
never grow up to sniff out drugs
or bombs

police dogs are fascist
and nobody worth a damn
likes fascism
which reminds me
don't let your dogs watch Fox News either
because no one loves a conservative dog

teach your dog to care
about the plight of less fortunate dogs
teach your dogs to have heart

and to have personality
let them slobber on the furniture
and beg for table scraps
tell them that
they're the best
good boy
on the whole fucking block
even
when it's not true

and love them
love them - love them
because with enough love
they'll never want to search cars for weed
to prove their own worth

Behind the 8 Ball Again

I've lived life
just like
I shoot pool

I'm not good at pool
because all I ever do
is focus
on this next shot
and I never think enough
about where
the cue ball
will come to rest

and too often
I leave
myself behind
the 8 ball again

so, I learned
how to jump
a cue ball

it's a wild shot
and not very effective
but when you're stuck
in another
dive bar pool game

or stuck in life
the worst thing
you can do
is nothing

and every once in a while
you'll make
an unbelievable shot
that's almost
enough
to make you forget
all the other shots
you've tried
and failed to make

Manufactured in China

another paycheck Friday
another paycheck that covers another week
but just so

work is work
dinner is dinner
ice cream sundaes are just ice cream sundaes

the American Dream is still out there
for $12.99
manufactured in China

I saw it on sale the other day
American Dreams 2 for $20
they had a big splashy -
spiky word balloon
on the front page of a sales flyer
for the local chain retail store
that is ran by a CEO
with a Wall Street heart
a heart
that's over inflated
approved by the senate
and growing colder
and smaller by the fiscal quarter
a chain retail store
that is ran by a CEO

with a Wall Street heart
sick from greed
and get rich quick cigarette schemes

heart-sick with the cancer
of American jobs given away
to the lowest bidders

and the CEO
with the Wall Street heart
has one blind eye and one deaf ear
so just enough to look out
for the war cries of revolution
and with a quiet sadness
the American worker
is left to work for peanuts
paper coupons with no cash value
and discount rack American Dreams
that used to be built here
but are now
only manufactured in China

All Out of Quarters in a Shopping Mall Arcade

there are no rules, man
none that make sense
like who says
I have to walk to the end of the block
to cross the street
or that I only need three weeks
to read this William Carlos Williams book
of poems
you hear me Toledo Library?
William Carlos William's poems knew
the rules didn't matter
and that time stands irrelevant

why do I have to pay for a happy meal
with five sad dollars
earned from 25 years
of not chasing my dreams
why can't I pay for a happy meal
with a happy dance
and a happy hug?

why don't we have paid
and professional cloud watchers
in every city park?
someone to lay back in the grass
and alert us of all of the interesting clouds

we never get to see
because blue skies are an afterthought
in the factory?

America
I'm tired of your silly games
I've been reading again
and Jesus was most assuredly a communist
Buddha was Buddha
pacifism through shared socialism
and Muhammad was nothing
if not a hedonist
and yet
we fight more than we fuck
and I'm tired of all the fighting, America

the matrix has been exposed
we're living life stuck in a video game
in a dying shopping mall arcade
a quarter at a time
I'm tired of working for quarters
and I don't want to play anymore

my heart has been broken a dozen times
but the thing that hurts the most
is how often I've forgotten
what happy feels like
except that I know
I've never found it
working a single overtime shift
in any factory

a famous monk gained enlightenment
then set himself on fire
and the world did not change for the better
Dr. King marched and gave everything
Harvey Milk did, too
for what?
to have their names put on street signs
in cities that are banned
from teaching critical race theory?
in cities where gay teens live
and still kill themselves at a four times higher rate?

I'm not a learned man
I don't know the answer to how to change the world
I can barely understand
how to read my electric bill
but the fucker
sure as shit
went up three months in a row
and I'm running
all out of quarters again
in this sad ass video game
in this dying shopping mall
in a midwestern city near you
and three hours
from everywhere else

Last Man Standing

sometimes I get so tired
that I think I might die
I don't die though
I just keep shuffling forward
with sand under my eyelids
with cracks in my kneecaps
with little nails stabbing my feet

they never said
that it'd be easy
but I'll be damned
if I ever heard 'em say
that it'd never be easy

I juggle pebbles all day
and count down minutes
when I sleep

I dream on my feet
and the winning lottery ticket
flutters away
like plastic grocery bags
being chased by a city street sweeper

my face is the mural of a poor man's life
my lungs are an ashtray
my heart is clogged with yesterday's dust

I was never promised a rose garden
but I didn't ask for this field of cockle-burrs
either

I would cry if it would wash away our sins

I would fly if I knew that we wouldn't crash

I would die a slow painful death if breathing
cost money

then again
the last man standing isn't always the winner

Dan Denton wrote poetry and short stories in the obscurity of rustbelt factories, and through a gauntlet of addictions, homelessness, rehabs and multiple divorces. His first poem was published at the age of 34, and at 36 he won the Toledo City Paper's annual poetry contest. Since then his work has appeared in countless zines, magazines, union trade journals, newspapers, and small press anthologies around the world, and he has been voted as the City of Toledo's best writer. He spent over 25 years laboring in the blue collar world, including a decade spent as a union autoworker, where he was fortunate to serve as an elected chief union steward, and as a constitutional delegate to the international UAW's annual bargaining and negotiating conventions. He took an early retirement for health concerns and to be able to spend more time writing, and now lives in an old, tiny travel trailer that he has dubbed "the Scrapes of Wrath." He is 18 years California sober.

This project was made possible, in part, by generous support from the Osage Arts Community.

Osage Arts Community provides temporary time, space and support for the creation of new artistic works in a retreat format, serving creative people of all kinds — visual artists, composers, poets, fiction and nonfiction writers. Located on a 152-acre farm in an isolated rural mountainside setting in Central Missouri and bordered by ¾ of a mile of the Gasconade River, OAC provides residencies to those working alone, as well as welcoming collaborative teams, offering living space and workspace in a country environment to emerging and mid-career artists. For more information, visit us at www.osageac.org

Osage Arts Community